the BATHROOM GOLF BOOK

By John Murphy

RED-LETTER PRESS, INC.
SADDLE RIVER, NEW JERSEY

Introduction and Acknowledgement

John Murphy, a veteran bathroomologist who's authored *The Bathroom Sports Quiz Book* and *The Bathroom Baseball Book,* has compiled the tantalizing trivia for this book. His latest sporting endeavor is teed up into nine question quizzes. Should you have trouble with the front nine, the back nine, or any nine in-between, you're encouraged to sit on it for awhile, enjoy the amusing quotes and facts, and then perhaps take another potshot at it.

A tip of the golf cap to those who've helped to produce this book and to place it where it belongs:

Cyndi Bellerose
Glenn Fraller
Sylvia Martin
Geoff Scowcroft

Yours flushingly,

Jack Kreismer
Publisher

Majors

1. Of all the players to ever win a Major, alphabetically who is last?

2. Who am I? In 1986, I led each professional Major after three rounds but won only one of them.

3. In which Major is only one course ever used?

4. The record for finishing in the top ten of Majors is 70. Who holds it?

5. The second best finisher in the top ten has done it 46 times. Name him.

6. What four men have won all four professional Majors?

7. Who was the first player to win the U.S. Open and the British Open in the same year?

8. What is the best one round score ever shot at a professional Major?

9. Who is the only left-handed player to ever win a professional Major?

It took me seventeen years to get three thousand hits. I did it in one afternoon on the golf course.
—Hank Aaron

1. *Fuzzy Zoeller.*

2. *Greg Norman. He "only" won the British Open.*

3. *The Masters.*

4. *Jack Nicklaus.*

5. *Sam Snead.*

6. *Gene Sarazen, Ben Hogan, Jack Nicklaus, and Gary Player.*

7. *Bobby Jones in 1926.*

8. *63. Coincidentally, it has been achieved at each of the four professional Majors.*

9. *Bob Charles.*

Thoughts of the Throne

Dave Stockton, complaining of the difficulty of playing Poppy Hills Golf Course in Pebble Beach, California, was heard to say: "Even the men's room has a double dogleg."

U.S. Open

1. Who was the last man to successfully defend his U.S. Open Championship?

2. Who was the previous man to win consecutive Opens?

3. Only one foreign-born player won the U.S. Open during the 1980's. Name him.

4. In the last forty years, two golfers with exactly four letters in their last names have won the tournament. Can you think of at least one of them?

5. In what year was the U.S. Open first held?

6. In 1960, this player birdied six of the last seven holes to win at Cherry Hills. Name him.

7. What player in a nine year span finished first or second eight times?

8. Who holds the record for the lowest 72 hole score at the Open?

9. The oldest player to win was 43 years 9 months old. Who is he?

I'm playing like Tarzan - and scoring like Jane.
—*Chi Chi Rodriguez*

1. *Curtis Strange in 1989.*

2. *Ben Hogan in 1950 and 1951.*

3. *David Graham in 1981.*

4. *Tommy Bolt in 1958 and Jerry Pate in 1976.*

5. *1895.*

6. *Arnold Palmer.*

7. *Bobby Jones from 1922 - 1930. He finished first four times, second four times, and eleventh on the other occasion.*

8. *Jack Nicklaus. He shot a 272 at Baltusrol in 1980.*

9. *Raymond Floyd at Shinnecock Hills in 1986.*

Equipment

1. Before the invention of wooden tees, what did golfers use to tee up the ball?

2. What Hall of Famer is credited with inventing the sand wedge?

3. The USGA recommends that the flagstick be at least how high?

4. What is the only club for which the grip does not have to be "generally circular"?

5. Do you know the brand golf ball which is used by more PGA tour pros than any other?

6. To the nearest inch, what is the diameter of a golf hole?

7. On average, how many golf balls does Tom Watson say that he uses in a round?

8. In the nineteenth century, most golf shafts were made of what wood?

9. In February, 1908, William Taylor took out a patent for making a certain type (not brand) of golf ball. What idea did he have for improving the ball?

I play in the low 80's. If it's any hotter than that, I won't play. —Joe E. Lewis

1.   *Sand. The golfer or his caddy would grab a pinch of wet sand from the sand box which was located near the tee area and form a makeshift pyramid. He would then place his ball on it.*

2.   *Gene Sarazen in the early 1930's.*

3.   *Seven feet.*

4.   *The putter.*

5.   *Titleist.*

6.   *Four inches. Since 1891, it is exactly four and one-fourth inches.*

7.   *Eight.*

8.   *Hickory.*

9.   *He put dimples on it to make the ball more accurate.*

Thoughts of the Throne

"I stayed at the club last year and my room was so clean, I didn't even want to take a shower."
—Lee Trevino, on the Riviera Golf Club,
Pacific Palisades, California

COLLEGES

Name the colleges attended by the following golfers.

1. Hale Irwin

2. Jack Nicklaus

3. Arnold Palmer

4. Scott Simpson

5. Craig Stadler

6. Curtis Strange

7. Lee Trevino

8. Tom Watson

9. Fuzzy Zoeller

Golf is a lot like taxes. You drive hard to get to the green, and then wind up in the hole.   *—Anonymous*

1. *Colorado.*

2. *Ohio State.*

3. *Wake Forest.*

4. *USC.*

5. *USC.*

6. *Wake Forest.*

7. *He did not attend college.*

8. *Stanford.*

9. *Houston.*

THE MASTERS

1. What golf club sponsors the Masters?

2. Which of the following is closest to the annual dues paid by each member of this prestigious club?
   - a) $2,000
   - b) $10,000
   - c) $50,000
   - d) $100,000

3. Name one of the four months in which the club is closed each year.

4. Who was the first president of this golf club?

5. Who will be the president in the year 2000?

6. In what month is the Masters played?

7. Who presents the green coat to the winner?

8. What winner was the first to receive a green coat? Hint: It was not the first winner.

9. Only one person is allowed to wear his green coat off the grounds of the club. Who?

I don't say my golf game is bad, but if I grew tomatoes, they'd come up sliced. **—Miller Barber**

1. *The Augusta National Golf Club.*

2. *a) $2,000. The money earned from the Masters Tournament provides most of the income needed to run the club. The initiation fee is approximately $20,000.*

3. *June, July, August, or September.*

4. *Bobby Jones.*

5. *Bobby Jones. In 1966, he was named "President in Perpetuity."*

6. *April.*

7. *The previous year's winner.*

8. *Sam Snead in 1949. At that time, all previous winners also received green coats.*

9. *The current winner of the Masters.*

CHIP SHOTS

Author Rudyard Kipling invented snow golf. The English writer, spending his winters in Vermont, painted his golf balls red in order to find them on snow covered courses.

BRITISH OPEN

1. Name the father-son duo which won eight of the first dozen British Opens.

2. In what year was the first British Open held?

3. Who won it?

4. What player won a record six British Opens?

5. On what golf course have the most British Opens been held?

6. In the last forty years, two players with exactly four letters in their last names have won this championship. Can you think of them both?
Hint: Both last names begin with the same letter.

7. Who won consecutive Opens in the 1980's?

8. The first American-born player to win the British Open did so in 1922. Name him.

9. Who was the first South African to win this title?

I've built golf courses and laid the irrigation system just by teeing off. **—Lee Trevino**

1.   *Old Tom Morris and Young Tom Morris.*

2.   *1860. Eight players entered and they played twelve holes three times each.*

3.   *Willie Park.*

4.   *Harry Vardon in 1896, 1898, 1899, 1903, 1911, and 1914.*

5.   *St. Andrews.*

6.   *Tony Lema in 1964 and Sandy Lyle in 1985.*

7.   *Tom Watson in 1982 and 1983.*

8.   *Walter Hagen.*

9.   *Bobby Locke.*

COURSES

1. In the last round of the 1982 U.S. Open, Tom Watson sank a pitch from the rough on the seventeenth hole to help him win the Championship. At what course was this Open played?

2. What golf course has Amen Corner?

3. In what year was the first golf course built in the Soviet Union?

4. What golf course has the famous Road Hole as its seventeenth?

5. The PGA Championship has been held at three public courses. Give one of them.

6. The AT&T Pebble Beach National Pro-Am Tournament (formerly the Crosby) is held at three golf courses. Obviously, one of them is Pebble Beach. Name the other two.

7. Who holds the 72 hole record for this tournament?

8. The British Open record for the lowest round at St. Andrews is 65. The course record is 62. What American holds it?

9. Since 1966, *Golf Digest* annually picks America's Top 10 courses. What Clementon, New Jersey, course has been on the list each year and is frequently named number 1?
Hint: The U.S. Open has never been held there but Walker Cup matches were in 1936 and 1985.

Golf does strange things to other people, too. It makes liars out of honest men, cheats out of altruists, cowards out of brave men and fools out of everybody. **—Milton Gross**

1. *Pebble Beach Golf Links.*

2. *Augusta National Golf Course.*

3. *1988.*

4. *St. Andrews in Scotland.*

5. *The Tanglewood Golf Club, North Carolina, 1974; Pebble Beach Golf Links, California, 1977; Kemper Lakes Golf Club, Illinois, 1989.*

6. *Spy Glass Hill and Cypress Point.*

7. *Tom Watson. He shot a 273 in 1977.*

8. *Curtis Strange.*

9. *Pine Valley Golf Club.*

CHIP SHOTS

President Dwight D. Eisenhower frequently practiced his putting on the grounds of the White House but was often interrupted by squirrels scurrying about the lawn. Ike remedied the problem by having his henchmen trap and remove the rascals.

PGA TOUR

1. Who is the first PGA player to shoot a score lower than his age in a round of a PGA tournament?

2. What is the record for most PGA tournaments won in a year?

3. Who holds this record?

4. Since 1950, who holds the record for most PGA events won in a year?

5. Only one man has won more than five PGA events in a year during the 1980's. Can you think of him?

6. What is the PGA record for consecutive birdies in a round?

7. Dewey Arnette is one of three men to accomplish this. Name one of the other two.

8. 27 years after winning a tournament event, this player won the same tournament. Name him.

9. Who is the last amateur to win a PGA event?

I don't like to watch golf on television. I can't stand whispering.   **—David Brenner**

1. *Sam Snead. In 1979, at the age of 67, he shot a 66 at the Quad Cities Open.*

2. *Eighteen.*

3. *Byron Nelson. He did it in 1945.*

4. *Sam Snead with ten.*

5. *Tom Watson. He won six in 1980.*

6. *Eight.*

7. *Bob Goalby in 1961 and Fuzzy Zoeller in 1976. Arnette did it in 1987.*

8. *Sam Snead. He won the Greensboro Open in 1938 and again in 1965. (He also won it in between.)*

9. *Scott Verplank. He won the 1985 Western Open.*

LPGA

1. What woman has the most LPGA tournament victories?

2. Who is second with 82 victories?

3. What Hall of Fame LPGA golfer is married to a baseball World Series MVP winner?

4. What Swede won the 1988 USGA Women's Open?

5. The lowest score for an LPGA 72 hole tournament is 268. Name the woman who did this at the 1985 Henreden Classic.

6. The last woman to successfully defend her U.S. Open title did so in 1978. Can you think of her?

7. What is the name of the trophy which is given to the LPGA player with the lowest average for the year?

8. One woman has won this trophy seven times. Name her.

9. Two others have won it five times each. Do you know either of them?

Eighteen holes of match or medal play will teach you more about your foe than will 18 years of dealing with him across a desk. **—Grantland Rice**

1.   *Kathy Whitworth - 88.*

2.   *Mickey Wright.*

3.   *Nancy Lopez. She is married to Ray Knight who won the award with the New York Mets in 1986.*

4.   *Liselotte Neumann.*

5.   *Nancy Lopez.*

6.   *Hollis Stacy.*

7.   *The Vare Trophy which is named after Glenna Collett Vare, a female star of the 1920's.*

8.   *Kathy Whitworth.*

9.   *Mickey Wright and JoAnne Carner.*

Thoughts of the Throne

". . . I've got to blow dry my hair or I've got to withdraw from the tournament. I don't play anywhere unless I can blow dry my hair."   —Ben Crenshaw

MEDIA

1. Name the golfer who has appeared on the cover of *Sports Illustrated* most frequently.

2. What Oscar-winning actor played in the 1950 British Amateur Tournament?

3. Can you remember the 1980's comedy movie involving golf which starred Rodney Dangerfield, Bill Murray, and Ted Knight?

4. Each year, *Sports Illustrated* gives a Sportsman of the Year Award. Can you name the two golfers who won this award during the 1970's?

5. Name the 1950's movie made about Ben Hogan.

6. Who played Hogan in this movie?

7. "Everyone in my family is talented: my father, my mother, my sister, Mary - she shot J.R.! Gosh, I *had* to win the Amateur." Can you name the 1981 U.S. Amateur winner who said this?

8. What two golfers won *Sports Illustrated* Sportsman of the Year Awards during the 1960's?

9. What actor who has a PGA Tour Event named after him authored *Confessions of a Hooker*?

Give me golf clubs, the fresh air and a beautiful partner and you can keep my golf clubs and the fresh air.
—Jack Benny

1. *Jack Nicklaus.*

2. *Bing Crosby. He lost in the first round 3 and 2.*

3. Caddyshack.

4. *Lee Trevino in 1971 and Jack Nicklaus in 1978.*

5. Follow the Sun.

6. *Glenn Ford.*

7. *Nathaniel Crosby (Bing's son).*

8. *Arnold Palmer in 1960 and Ken Venturi in 1964.*

9. *Bob Hope.*

RYDER CUP

1. Who plays in the Ryder Cup matches — professionals, amateurs, or both?

2. How frequently are the matches held?

3. In what year did the Ryder Cup competition start?

4. What two conditions must you meet to play a Ryder Cup match for your country?

5. How are the members of the United States team picked?

6. Prior to 1979, what countries played for the Ryder Cup?

7. Since 1979, what countries play for the Cup?

8. In what year did the United States team lose on home ground for the first time?

9. What Hall of Famer has been selected as captain of the American team the most?

I'd give up golf if I didn't have so many sweaters.
—Bob Hope

1. *Professionals.*

2. *The matches are held every other year on a home-and-home basis.*

3. *It started in 1927. The Cup was donated by Samuel A. Ryder, a wealthy seed merchant from England.*

4. *You must be a native-born citizen of your country and you must be a member of your country's PGA.*

5. *The American team is picked by total number of points earned in PGA Tour events.*

6. *The United States against Great Britain and later Great Britain and Ireland. In 24 matches against these countries, the United States won 20 and tied one.*

7. *The United States versus a combined team of European players.*

8. *In 1987. The European team beat them at Muirfield Golf Club in Ohio.*

9. *Walter Hagen — seven times.*

CHIP SHOTS

The usage of the word "green" in golf originally stood for the whole course, thus the meaning of such terms as "green fees" and "greenkeeper." The official term for what is now known as the green is the "putting green."

FOREIGN-BORN

Each of the following players was born outside of the United States. Name the country.

1. Isao Aoki

2. Seve Ballesteros

3. T.C. Chen

4. Nick Faldo

5. David Graham

6. Bernhard Langer

7. Sandy Lyle

8. Greg Norman

9. Nick Price

The average expert player — if he is lucky — hits six, eight or ten real good shots in a round. The rest are good misses.   *—Tommy Armour*

1. *Japan.*

2. *Spain.*

3. *Taiwan.*

4. *England.*

5. *Australia.*

6. *West Germany.*

7. *Scotland.*

8. *Australia.*

9. *South Africa.*

MONEY

1. Who was the first man to make a million dollars on the PGA Tour during his career?

2. Who was the first to reach the five million dollar mark?

3. 1988 was the first year that a player made a million dollars on the PGA Tour. Name him.

4. In what decade did the entire tour prize money for a year first reach a million dollars?

5. In the 1970's, only four players were the leading money winners of the year. How many can you get?

6. Who are the only two brothers to have each won more than $1.5 million on the PGA Tour?

7. Of all the players who have never won a Major, who has won the most money on the PGA Tour?

8. What man has been the leading money winner on the tour the most times?

9. Who was the first woman to win a million dollars on the LPGA Tour during her career?

Golf is like a love affair: If you don't take it seriously, it's no fun; if you do take it seriously, it breaks your heart. —*Arnold Daly*

1. *Arnold Palmer.*

2. *Jack Nicklaus.*

3. *Curtis Strange.*

4. *The 1950's. It reached the one million dollar mark in 1958, the ten million dollar mark in 1979, and the twenty million dollar mark in 1985.*

5. *Johnny Miller, Jack Nicklaus, Lee Trevino, and Tom Watson.*

6. *Bobby and Lanny Wadkins.*

7. *Tom Kite.*

8. *Jack Nicklaus — eight.*

9. *Kathy Whitworth.*

Thoughts of the Throne

Joyce Kazmierski, on network television at the 1983 Women's Kemper Open, said this about weather conditions: "The wind was so strong there were whitecaps in the porta-john."

NICKNAMES

Can you identify these golfers?

1. The Walrus

2. The Golden Bear

3. The White Shark

4. Mr. X

5. Slammin'

6. The Machine

7. The Merry Mex

8. Doc

9. The Hawk

If a lot of people gripped a knife and fork like they do a golf club, they'd starve to death.   **—Sam Snead**

1. *Craig Stadler.*

2. *Jack Nicklaus.*

3. *Greg Norman.*

4. *Miller Barber.*

5. *Sam Snead.*

6. *Gene Littler.*

7. *Lee Trevino.*

8. *Cary Middlecoff.*

9. *Ben Hogan.*

THE MASTERS

1. What golfer has won the most Masters?

2. How many times has he won it?

3. The second most frequent winner of this tournament has won it four times. Who is he?

4. The first winner of the Masters has the initials H.S. Do you know him?

5. In what year was the Masters first held?

6. Who am I? A three-time Masters champ, I appeared on the cover of *Golf* magazine's first issue in April, 1959.

7. In the last 40 years, four players with exactly four letters in their last names have been winners. How many do you know?

8. Only one golfer won two Masters in the 1980's. Name him.

9. The record for playing in the most Masters is 44. What Hall of Famer holds the mark?

What other people may find in poetry or art museums, I find in the flight of a good drive — the white ball sailing up into the blue sky, growing smaller and smaller, then suddenly reaching its apex, curving, falling and finally dropping to the turf to roll some more, just the way I planned it.
Arnold Palmer

1. *Jack Nicklaus.*

2. *Six. He won it in 1963, '65, '66, '72, '75, and '86.*

3. *Arnold Palmer — in 1958, '60, '62, and '64.*

4. *Horton Smith. He also won the third Masters.*

5. *1934.*

6. *Jimmy Demaret.*

7. *Doug Ford, 1957; Art Wall, Jr., 1959; Larry Mize, 1987; and Sandy Lyle, 1988.*

8. *Seve Ballesteros in 1980 and 1983.*

9. *Sam Snead.*

CHIP SHOTS

A golf ball can travel as fast as 170.5 miles per hour. The average duffer can drive a ball which will achieve an initial speed of 125 miles per hour.

U.S. OPEN

1. What player shot a record 63 in the final round to win the Open?

2. Two other players shot 63's in the Open. Coincidentally, both did it in the opening round of the 1980 Open. Who were they?

3. In the 1980's, there were two playoffs. Name the two winners and the two losers.

4. Only three players have competed in over thirty consecutive U.S. Opens. Give two of them.

5. This Englishman was the only foreign-born winner of the Championship in the 1970's. Who is he?

6. The previous Englishman to win the U.S. Open did so exactly a half-century before. Can you think of him?

7. What golfer lost three playoffs for the Open in the 1960's?

8. Can you name one of the players who beat him?

9. I'm thinking of a player who had only one victory during the 1950's and that was in a playoff with Ben Hogan for the 1955 U.S. Open. Name him.

You must expect anything in golf. A stranger comes through, he's keen for a game, he seems affable enough, and on the eighth fairway he turns out to be an idiot. —Alistair Cooke

1.   *Johnny Miller in 1973 at Oakmont.*

2.   *Jack Nicklaus and Tom Weiskopf at Baltusrol.*

3.   *In 1984, Fuzzy Zoeller beat Greg Norman; in 1988, Curtis Strange defeated Nick Faldo.*

4.   *Jack Nicklaus, Arnold Palmer, and Gene Sarazen.*

5.   *Tony Jacklin in 1970.*

6.   *Edward "Ted" Ray in 1920.*

7.   *Arnold Palmer in 1962, 1963, and 1966.*

8.   *Jack Nicklaus, 1962; Julius Boros, 1963; and Billy Casper, Jr. in 1966.*

9.   *Jack Fleck.*

SCORING

1. What player is awarded the Vardon Trophy each year?

2. Two players have won this trophy five times each. Do you know either one?

3. Who won the Vardon Trophy in 1977, 1978, and 1979?

4. Only one foreign-born player won the trophy twice. Who?

5. Who's the only black to have won the Vardon Trophy?

6. In 1987, David Frost won over a half million dollars and had the best average on the PGA Tour but did not win the Vardon Trophy. Why not?

7. From 1960 to 1968, only two players led the PGA in scoring. Name both of them.

8. Who had the best 72 hole score in a PGA event?

9. What was his total?

Once when I was golfing in Georgia I hooked the ball into the swamp. I went in after it and found an alligator wearing a shirt with a picture of a little golfer on it.
                                        —Buddy Hackett

1.   *The PGA member who has the best scoring average on the Tour that year.*

2.   *Billy Casper and Lee Trevino.*

3.   *Tom Watson.*

4.   *Bruce Crampton in 1973 and 1975.*

5.   *Calvin Peete in 1984.*

6.   *He was not a member of the PGA.*

7.   *Arnold Palmer in 1961, '62, '64, and '67; Billy Casper in 1960, '63, '65, '66, and '68.*

8.   *Mike Souchak at the 1955 Texas Open.*

9.   *257 (60-68-64-65).*

Thoughts of the Throne

On the go on the LPGA tour — Vicki Tabor, Debbie Hall, Alexandra Reinhard and Kathryn Young have a superstition in common. If they're playing well in a particular tournament, they keep using the same bathroom stall in the locker room. If the stall is occupied, well, they just consider waiting time to be a part of the game.

PGA CHAMPIONSHIP

1. What golfer won four consecutive PGA championships?

2. The best score for a round at the PGA is a 63. Give one of the three players to shoot this.

3. In what year did they hold the first PGA championship?

4. It was held in Bronxville, New York. At what country club?

5. Who was the winner?

6. In what decade did the PGA switch from match play to stroke play?

7. In 1953, Ben Hogan won the Masters, U.S. Open, and the British Open. Why couldn't he have won the PGA?

8. There have been three golfers within the last forty years who have won the PGA championship and have exactly four letters in their last names. Give two of them.

9. Who is the oldest man to win the PGA championship?

The only reason I played golf was so I could afford to go fishing and hunting.   **—Sam Snead**

1. *Walter Hagen, 1924 - 1927.*

2. *Bruce Crampton, 1975; Raymond Floyd, 1982; and Gary Player, 1984.*

3. *1916.*

4. *Siwanoy Country Club.*

5. *Long Jim Barnes. In fact, he also won the second one which was held in 1919.*

6. *The 1950's. 1957 was the last championship decided by match play.*

7. *It took place in the same week as the British Open.*

8. *Doug Ford, 1955; Dave Marr, 1965; and Bob Tway, 1986.*

9. *Julius Boros. He was 48 when he won in 1968.*

SENIOR PGA TOUR

1. In what year did the Senior PGA Tour begin? How old do you have to be to play in it?

2. What foreign-born player won the first USGA Senior Open?

3. He never won a Major on the regular tour, yet captured three of the first six USGA Senior Opens. Who is he?

4. The 1970 National Football League MVP has won over a quarter of a million dollars on the Senior Tour. Can you think of him or do you want to pass on this question?

5. Who was the first man to win both the U.S. Open and Senior Open?

6. Name the first player to win a senior PGA tournament without ever winning on the regular tour.

7. Who was the first player to win a million dollars on the Senior Tour?

8. Can you name the senior golfer who got eight consecutive birdies in the 1987 Silver Pages Classic?

9. What was Lee Trevino referring to when he called it "the biggest mulligan in golf"?

I'm hitting the woods just great, but I'm having a terrible time getting out of them.   **—Harry Toscano**

1. *It began in 1980 with two tournaments. You must be 50 to play in it.*

2. *Roberto DeVicenzo at the Winged Foot Golf Club in 1980.*

3. *Miller Barber who won it in 1982, 1984, and 1985.*

4. *John Brodie of the San Francisco 49ers.*

5. *Arnold Palmer. He won the second Senior Open.*

6. *Walter Zembriski who won the Newport Cup Tournament in 1988.*

7. *Don January in 1985. He has actually made more money on the Senior Tour than he did on the regular tour.*

8. *Chi Chi Rodriguez.*

9. *The Senior Tour.*

CHIP SHOTS

The clubhead of a driver, when it strikes the ball, remains in contact with it for half-a-thousandth of a second and stays with the ball for three quarters of an inch.

RULES

Decide whether each of the following is legal or illegal. If illegal, give the penalty in stroke play.

1. I ask you what club you just hit.

2. Just before putting on the green, I use my club to flatten a few spike marks which are on my line.

3. I'm closer to the hole than you are, but hit first.

4. With my ball in a sand trap, I touch the sand with my club to determine its condition.

5. I swing at a ball and top it and when it is in the air my club strikes it a second time.

6. My ball is in the fairway and a loose twig is touching it. I pick the twig up and, in the process, my ball moves.

7. A candy wrapper is lying on my ball in the fairway. As I pick the wrapper up, my ball moves.

8. I hit a shot which accidentally hits my golf cart.

9. My ball is overhanging the lip of the cup and I wait two minutes. At that point, the ball falls into the cup.

Middle age occurs when you are too young to take up golf and too old to rush up to the net.
—Franklin Pierce Adams

1. *Illegal - two stroke penalty. If you answer me, you also get a two stroke penalty.*

2. *Illegal - two stroke penalty.*

3. *No penalty - the ball shall be played where it lies.*

4. *Illegal - two stroke penalty.*

5. *Illegal - one stroke penalty. If you were lying three before your first swing, you now lie five. (This situation actually happened to T.C. Chen at the 1985 U.S. Open.)*

6. *Illegal - one stroke penalty.*

7. *No penalty - a candy wrapper is not a natural object.*

8. *Illegal - two stroke penalty. Play the ball where it lies.*

9. *Illegal - one stroke penalty. If the putt was my fourth shot, I get a five for the hole.*

BRITISH OPEN

1. Many consider the 1977 British Open at Turnberry to be one of the all-time best. Tied for the lead after two rounds, two players played the last 36 holes together. The older one shot a score seven strokes better than the previous Open record. The younger one was one stroke better and won his second title. Name these two great players.

2. That 1977 score is still the record for the lowest 72 hole score at the Open. What is it?

3. Who won consecutive British Opens in the 1970's?

4. At what course were the first twelve Opens held?

5. What two Americans each won back-to-back British Opens in the 1920's?

6. Who was the oldest winner of the Open?

7. Who was the youngest?

8. Only one American has ever won five British Opens. Can you name him?

9. In the 1983 championship, this American missed a three inch putt and eventually lost the Open by one stroke. Who suffered this fate?

I'm glad we don't have to play in the shade.
—Bobby Jones, when told it was 105 degrees
in the shade

1. *Tom Watson beat Jack Nicklaus.*

2. *268.*

3. *Lee Trevino in 1977 and 1978.*

4. *Prestwick in Aryshire, Scotland.*

5. *Bobby Jones in 1926 and 1927; Walter Hagen in 1928 and 1929.*

6. *Old Tom Morris — he was 46.*

7. *Young Tom Morris — he was 17. Tragically, he died when he was 24.*

8. *Tom Watson.*

9. *Hale Irwin. He tried to tap the ball in with a backhand stroke and missed it.*

Thoughts of the Throne

While on the PGA tour in 1968, Lee Trevino visited the Alamo in San Antonio, Texas, after which SuperMex was heard to say, "Well, I'm not gonna buy this place. It doesn't have indoor plumbing."

CLUBS AND COURSES

1. What golf club is considered to be the oldest American golf club in continuous operation?

2. The oldest golf club in North America is located in what Canadian city?

3. Five golf clubs were charter members of the USGA when it was founded in 1894. Can you think of three of them?

4. At which one of these five clubs was the first U.S. Open held?

5. Which one of these five clubs had the first 18 hole course in the United States?

6. What U.S. city had the first municipal golf course?

7. Which golf club is acknowledged as the oldest in the world?

8. If a Scotsman says that he is a member of the R & A, to what is he referring? (Specifically, what do the letters R & A stand for?)

9. Excluding the British Isles, what country had the first golf course?

I like to say I was born on the nineteenth hole — the only one I ever parred.   *—George Low*

1. *St. Andrews of Hastings-on-Hudson, New York. It was founded on November 14, 1888. (The club was originally based in Yonkers, New York.)*

2. *Montreal. The Royal Montreal Golf Club was founded in 1873.*

3. *St. Andrews Golf Club; The Country Club (in Brookline, MA); Shinnecock Hills Golf Club; Newport Golf Club; and Chicago Golf Club.*

4. *The Newport Golf Club.*

5. *The Chicago Golf Club in 1894.*

6. *New York City. Van Cortlandt Golf Course was founded in the Bronx in 1895. It is still in operation.*

7. *Honourable Company of Edinburgh Golfers based at Muirfield, Scotland. They are the descendants of the Gentlemen Golfers which was recognized by the Edinburgh Town Council in 1744 (ten years before St. Andrews).*

8. *The Royal & Ancient Golf Club of St. Andrews. This title was conferred by King William IV of Scotland in 1834.*

9. *India in 1829 — The Royal Calcutta Golf Club.*

U.S. OPEN

1. In 1968, this man was the first to shoot four sub-70 rounds at the same U.S. Open. Who?

2. The lowest score ever shot by an amateur at the Open is 282. Who accomplished this?

3. Do you know the first American-born player to win the U.S. Open?

4. Only one player has ever had a double eagle at this tournament. The year was 1985. Who?

5. Who was the only foreign-born player to win the Open in the 1960's?

6. What golfer during the 1960's lost a seven stroke lead on the last nine holes and then lost in a playoff the next day?

7. There was only one two-time winner in the 1970's. Can you think of him?

8. Who's the only U.S. Open winner to have also won the U.S. Junior Amateur title?

9. The answer to one of the above questions is also the youngest man ever to win the Open. Who?

Gary Player is all right if you like to see a grown man dressed up like Black Bart all the time.
—Don Rickles

1.   *Lee Trevino at Oak Hill. He shot 69-68-69-69.*

2.   *Jack Nicklaus in 1960.*

3.   *John J. McDermott in 1911.*

4.   *T.C. Chen. He got a deuce at a par 5 at Oakland Hills.*

5.   *Gary Player in 1965 at the Bellerive Country Club.*

6.   *Arnold Palmer in 1966 at the Olympic Club. In fact, he still had a six stroke lead with six holes to go. In the next day's playoff, he led by two after nine, but lost 69-73 to Billy Casper.*

7.   *Hale Irwin in 1974 and 1979.*

8.   *Johnny Miller.*

9.   *John J. McDermott in 1911. He was 19 years, 10 months old.*

CHIP SHOTS

Golfers are a superstitious lot and Tom Watson is no exception. Admittedly afraid of the bogey man, Watson always carries three coins in his pocket and three tees. On par 3 holes, he uses a broken tee. If he happens to shoot a good round, he'll have the same thing for dinner that he had the night before.

U.S. PRESIDENTS

1. Who was our first golfing President?

2. What President was a member of the Augusta National Golf Club?

3. Name the first President to have a public golf course named after him.

4. What President's father was president of the U.S. Golf Association?

5. "I know I'm getting better at golf because I'm hitting fewer spectators." What President said this?

6. Who am I? My grandfather was the "Walker" for whom the Walker Cup was named?

7. What chief executive who had been president of Princeton University played golf at least once a week?

8. Not all of our Presidents played golf. What taciturn President, when asked why he didn't play golf said, "I do not see the sense in chasing a little white ball around a field."

9. Who is the only President to hold an honorary membership on the PGA Tour?

Have you ever noticed what golf spells backwards?
—Al Boliska

1. *William Howard Taft (1909 - 1913) who played at least once a week.*

2. *Dwight Eisenhower.*

3. *Warren G. Harding. The course is in San Francisco.*

4. *George Bush. His father, Prescott Bush, later a U.S. Senator, was president of the USGA in the 1930's.*

5. *Gerald Ford in 1984.*

6. *George Herbert Walker Bush. His maternal grandfather, George Herbert Walker, was president of the USGA in the 1920's.*

7. *Woodrow Wilson.*

8. *Calvin Coolidge.*

9. *Gerald Ford.*

THE MASTERS

1. Who was the first foreign-born player to win the Masters?

2. In the 1980's, foreign-born players won it five times. Can you name the four different players?

3. The record for the lowest 18 hole score at the tournament is 63. What South African-born player did this in 1986?

4. The record score for the tournament is 271. Two players have accomplished this. Give at least one of them.

5. What amateurs have won the Masters?

6. What amateur led the 1956 tournament after three rounds and shot an 80 on the last day to lose by one stroke? Hint: Eight years later, he won the U.S. Open.

7. Who is the only man to successfully defend his title?

8. Who was the first black to play at the Masters?

9. Besides Nicklaus, what other player won two Masters during the 1970's?

Golf and sex are about the only things you can enjoy without being good at. **—Jimmy Demaret**

1.   *Gary Player in 1961.*

2.   *Seve Ballesteros, Bernhard Langer, Sandy Lyle, and Nick Faldo.*

3.   *Nick Price.*

4.   *Jack Nicklaus in 1965 and Raymond Floyd in 1976.*

5.   *No amateur has ever won the Masters.*

6.   *Ken Venturi. He led by four going into the last round and finished one behind the winner, Jack Burke.*

7.   *Jack Nicklaus in 1966.*

8.   *Lee Elder in 1975.*

9.   *Gary Player in 1974 and 1978.*

Thoughts of the Throne

I love to sweat and heave and breathe and hurt and burn and get dirty . . . There's something good about getting all dirty and grimy and nasty and then showering; you feel twice as clean.   —*Jan Stephenson*

PGA TOUR

1. In 1945, these three golfers won 29 of the 35 events. Give all three.

2. Who holds the tour record for career wins?

3. What foreign-born player has the most victories on the PGA Tour?

4. What is the oldest event on the PGA Tour?

5. The tournament held at Benton Harbor, Michigan, is the second oldest event. It started in 1899. What is it?

6. How many years ago did Arnold Palmer win his last regular PGA event?

7. Who won the first PGA event with a colored ball?

8. The PGA record for winning the same event the most times is eight. Who holds this record?

9. What event did he win eight times?

A lot of guys who have never choked, have never been in the position to do so. **—Tom Watson**

1. *Ben Hogan, Byron Nelson, and Sam Snead.*

2. *Sam Snead. He has won 84.*

3. *Gary Player, 21.*

4. *The U.S. Open.*

5. *The Western Open.*

6. *His last victory was at the 1973 Bob Hope Desert Classic at the age of 43.*

7. *Wayne Levi at the 1982 Hawaiian Open. He used a yellow ball.*

8. *Sam Snead.*

9. *The Greensboro Open in 1938, '46, '49, '50, '55, '56, '60, and '65.*

BOBBY JONES

1. Bobby Jones won his native state's amateur title at the age of fourteen. What is his native state?

2. What was his middle name?

3. Which two Majors did he not win?

4. In what year did he win the Grand Slam?

5. What four events comprised the Grand Slam when he won it?

6. How old was Jones when he retired?

7. Name one of the two colleges which he attended as an undergraduate.

8. What was his occupation?

9. What nickname did he give his putter?

All my life I wanted to play golf like Jack Nicklaus, and now I do.   *—Paul Harvey,*
after Jack Nicklaus shot
a first round 83 at the British Open in 1981

1.   *Georgia.*

2.   *Tyre. His full name was Robert Tyre Jones, Jr.*

3.   *The Masters and the PGA Championship.*

4.   *1930.*

5.   *The U.S. Open, British Open, U.S. Amateur, and British Amateur.*

6.   *28.*

7.   *Georgia Tech and Harvard.*

8.   *Lawyer.*

9.   *Calamity Jane.*

CHIP SHOTS

Obsessed as they are about golf, in Tokyo the Japanese play the sport in "chicken-coops" which are 6½ foot cubicles tiered by the hundreds on top of a skyscraper. It is in this coop where one can practice driving the ball — the only golf available in the crowded city.

EQUIPMENT

1. What is the maximum number of clubs you're allowed to carry in a golf match?

2. What's the penalty in stroke play for having an extra club?

3. During a match, your driver breaks after hitting a ball. Are you allowed to replace it?

4. A featherie was used by golfers until about 1850. What is a featherie?

5. What is a gutta percha?

6. To the nearest hundred, how many dimples are on most modern golf balls?

7. A golf hole should be how many inches deep?

8. What is the diameter of an American golf ball?

9. If when swinging at a ball, you cut it, are you allowed to immediately replace it?

Golf is the most fun you can have without taking your clothes off. —**Chi Chi Rodriguez**

1. *Fourteen. This rule went into effect in 1938. During the early 1930's, some golfers carried as many as 25 clubs in a match. Quite a bagful compared to Francis Ouimet who won the 1913 U.S. Open with only seven clubs.*

2. *You are penalized two strokes for every hole for which you had the extra club with a maximum penalty of four strokes. After discovering that you have an extra club, you are disqualified if you do not discard it.*

3. *Yes, as long as you do not delay play. On the other hand, had you broken the club in a fit of anger, you would not be permitted to replace it.*

4. *A golf ball. It was made by filling a leather sack with a bucket of wet goose feathers. When the feathers dried, they expanded and made the ball hard. Today, an original featherie sells for about $4,000.*

5. *A rubber-like ball which replaced the featherie.*

6. *400.*

7. *Four.*

8. *1.68 inches.*

9. *Yes.*

COLLEGES

1. From its inaugural year in 1897 until 1933, the NCAA Division 1 Golf Team Champions were all from what conference?

2. From 1949 to 1972, colleges from this state won 19 of the 24 NCAA Division 1 golf championships.

3. What Ohio State player was the college champion in 1961?

4. Since World War II, which college has won the most team Championships?

5. Who am I? From 1971 - 1973, I won three consecutive NCAA Division 1 titles and later won a Major.

6. What college did this triple-winner attend?

7. What teammate of his tied with him for the individual championship in 1972?

8. From 1986 to 1988, three different players from Oklahoma State won NCAA individual championships. Give one of these three players.

9. What college has won the most NCAA Division 1 Team Golf Championships?

My best score ever is 103, but I've only been playing 15 years. —*Alex Karras*

1.   *The Ivy League.*

2.   *Texas. Four different colleges won - North Texas State, SMU, Houston, and Texas.*

3.   *Jack Nicklaus.*

4.   *Houston - 16.*

5.   *Ben Crenshaw.*

6.   *Texas.*

7.   *Tom Kite.*

8.   *Scott Verplank, 1986; Brian Watts, 1987; and E.J. Pfister, 1988.*

9.   *Yale, 21.*

Thoughts of the Throne

Dave Hill, in his book *Teed Off,* has this to say about the ever popular Arnold Palmer: "The tournament brass will stop at nothing to keep Palmer happy. There is a story that he left the eleventh fairway one year to go into the woods and relieve himself. The next year a permanent restroom had been built on the spot."

U.S. OPEN

Match the following years with the events listed below:

1902	1922	1943
1909	1931	1954
1916	1933	1965

1. Last time the U.S. Open is won by an amateur.

2. First time the Open is scheduled for four days.

3. First time four sub-80 rounds are shot at the same U.S. Open.

4. First time a sub-70 round is shot.

5. Winner plays 144 holes of golf.

6. First time admission is charged to watch the Open.

7. First time it is televised nationally.

8. First time total prize money exceeded one thousand dollars.

9. No winner of the tournament.

I always keep a supply of stimulants handy in case I see a snake, which I also keep handy. —W.C. Fields, as he put whiskey in his golf bag

1.   *1933. John Goodman won it.*

2.   *1965. Previously, the last 36 holes were played on Saturday.*

3.   *1902. Laurence Auchterlonie shot 78-78-74-77 to win the tournament by six strokes.*

4.   *1909. Dave Hunter shot a 68 in the first round.*

5.   *1931. Billy Burke and George Von Elm tied after regulation 72 holes, tied after a playoff 36 holes, and finally decided the match after another 36 hole playoff. Burke won by one stroke.*

6.   *1922.*

7.   *1954.*

8.   *1916.*

9.   *1943. The Open was cancelled because of World War II.*

LPGA

1. Who am I? I won the U.S. Women's Open in golf in 1967 and my father won the U.S. Open in tennis twice.

2. What Japanese player won the 1987 LPGA Player of the Year Award?

3. Who is the oldest winner of an LPGA tournament?

4. The lowest scoring average for a season by an LPGA player is 70.73. Name her.

5. This 1932 Gold Medal winner at the Olympics later won three U.S. Women's Opens. Can you think of her?

6. What was this woman's real first name?

7. Who was the first Australian to win an LPGA Major?

8. "Big Mama" is the nickname of what golfer?

9. The record for most women's Majors is nine. What golfer has done this?

Rail-splitting produced an immortal president in Abraham Lincoln; but golf, with 29,000 courses, hasn't produced even a good A-Number-1 congressman.   —*Will Rogers*

1. *Catherine Lacoste. Her father, René Lacoste, won the U.S. Open tennis championship in 1926 and 1927.*

2. *Ayako Okamoto.*

3. *JoAnne Carner. She won the 1985 Safeco Classic when she was 46 years old.*

4. *Nancy Lopez in 1985.*

5. *Babe Didrikson Zaharias.*

6. *Mildred.*

7. *Jan Stephenson. She won the LPGA Championship in 1982.*

8. *JoAnne Carner.*

9. *Mickey Wright.*

CHIP SHOTS

The St. Louis *Post-Dispatch* once featured this sporting headline:
Shot Off Woman's Leg Helps Nicklaus To 66

NAMES

1. What is Fuzzy Zoeller's real name?

2. Who is the first woman golfer that we know by name?

3. The "National Invitation Tournament" was the original name of what golf tournament?

4. "I just got an albatross on that hole." What would a Britisher mean if he used these words?

5. Only one player with exactly three letters in his last name has ever won a Major. Can you think of him?

6. What is the real first name of Chi Chi Rodriguez?

7. Who were the "Gold Dust Twins?"

8. If sixty years ago, a Britisher said that he had gotten a bogie on a hole, what would he have meant?

9. In the rulebook, the phrase "through the green" comes up frequently. What does this phrase mean?

He's like a young Toots Shor — a victim of circumference. —Jimmy Demaret, *on the appearance of young Jack Nicklaus*

1.   *Frank Urban Zoeller, hence the nickname Fuzzy.*

2.   *Mary, Queen of Scots. Historians wrote that she was seen playing golf a few days after her husband had been murdered in 1567.*

3.   *The Masters.*

4.   *He had just gotten a double eagle.*

5.   *Edward "Ted" Ray.*

6.   *Juan.*

7.   *Byron Nelson and Harold "Jug" McSpaden.*

8.   *He would have meant what we do today when we say that we got a par.*

9.   *It means the entire course except the teeing ground, the putting green, and all hazards. Out-of-bounds is, of course, not considered to be part of the course.*

PGA CHAMPIONSHIP

1. What brothers won the PGA Championship within the past forty years?

2. Who was the first American to win the PGA?

3. In what year was the PGA of America founded?

4. What is the name of the trophy given to the winner of the PGA? Hint: It was donated by the son of a department store magnate.

5. The best 72 hole score ever shot at the PGA was 271. Name the golfer who did this in 1964.

6. Two men have won five PGA titles each. Give them both.

7. Who is the only player to win two PGA titles during the 1980's?

8. These two players won seven of the first ten PGA Championships. Can you get them both?

9. True or False: In the last half-century, no one has won back to back PGA titles.

For most amateurs, the best wood in the bag is the pencil.   *—Chi Chi Rodriguez*

1.   *Jay Hebert in 1957 and Lionel Hebert in 1960.*

2.   *Walter Hagen in 1921.*

3.   *It was founded on January 16, 1916.*

4.   *The Wanamaker Trophy.*

5.   *Bobby Nichols at the Columbus Country Club in Columbus, Ohio.*

6.   *Walter Hagen and Jack Nicklaus.*

7.   *Larry Nelson in 1981 and 1987.*

8.   *Walter Hagen and Gene Sarazen.*

9.   *True.*

Thoughts of the Throne

When golfer Johnny Pott was introduced at the Los Angeles Open in the 1960's, the announcer committed this blooper: "Now on the pot, Johnny Tee."

ONE AND ONLY

Each of the following golfers has won exactly one professional Major. Name it.

1. Charles Coody

2. Ben Crenshaw

3. Roberto DeVicenzo

4. Don January

5. Johnny Miller

6. Orville Moody

7. Craig Stadler

8. Hal Sutton

9. Tom Weiskopf

My family was so poor they couldn't afford any kids.
The lady next door had me. **—Lee Trevino**

1.   *The Masters in 1971.*

2.   *The Masters in 1984.*

3.   *The British Open in 1967.*

4.   *The PGA Championship in 1967.*

5.   *The U.S. Open in 1970.*

6.   *The U.S. Open in 1969.*

7.   *The Masters in 1982.*

8.   *The PGA Championship in 1983.*

9.   *The British Open in 1973.*

THE MASTERS

1. Most people agree that the most famous golf shot at the Masters was the 4 wood hit on the fifteenth hole in the last round of the 1935 Masters by the eventual winner of the tournament. Who was he?

2. What did he score on the hole?

3. As a result of this shot, what golfer did he tie and eventually beat the next day in a 36 hole playoff?

4. Another famous Masters occurred in 1968 when a player who would have tied for the lead handed in a signed scorecard on the last day with an incorrectly posted score. The scorecard showed that he'd gotten a 4 on the seventeenth hole when it was really a 3. Who was this player?

5. What was the ruling?

6. What would the ruling have been had he written a 2 instead of a 4?

7. Who was this golfer's playing partner and the one who actually wrote the 4 on the scorecard?

8. Who won the tournament?

9. Final history question: did Bobby Jones ever play in the Masters?

If you've got to remind yourself to concentrate during competition, you've got no chance to concentrate. **—Bobby Nichols**

1. *Gene Sarazen.*

2. *A double eagle two on the par five 485 yard hole. His shot went approximately 220 yards.*

3. *Craig Wood. He beat him by five strokes.*

4. *Roberto DeVicenzo.*

5. *He was credited with a 4. As a result, he finished in second place.*

6. *He would have been disqualified from the tournament. If you write a score higher than what you really got, you are credited with this score; if you write a lower score, you're disqualified.*

7. *Tommy Aaron. The pros frequently keep the scorecard for their playing partner; the card becomes official when it is signed and handed in.*

8. *Bob Goalby.*

9. *Yes. In fact, he played in the first and finished thirteenth. (This was his first tournament play in four years.)*

CHIP SHOTS

The longest hole in one ever belongs to Bob Mutera as he recorded an ace on the downhill, 10th hole at Miracle Hill Golf Course in Omaha, Nebraska, in 1965. The distance — 447 yards.

WALKER AND CURTIS CUPS

1. Who plays in the Walker and Curtis Cup Matches — professionals, amateurs, or both?

2. What countries play in these competitions?

3. How frequently are the matches held?

4. In what decade did the Walker Cup Matches begin?

5. How many matches has the United States lost?

6. In what decade did the Curtis Cup Matches begin?

7. In what year did the United States first lose a Curtis Cup Match on home ground?

8. If a match is tied, which country keeps each Cup?

9. What Walker Cup participant had a son who won 300 games as a pitcher in baseball?

By the time you get dressed, drive out there, play 18 holes, and come home, you've blown seven hours. There are better things you can do with your time.
—President Richard M. Nixon

1.   *Amateurs. Men play for the Walker Cup; women for the Curtis Cup.*

2.   *The United States versus the British Isles (i.e., Great Britain and Ireland).*

3.   *The matches are held every other year on a home-and-home basis.*

4.   *The 1920's. The first match was held in 1922.*

5.   *Three. The last time was in 1989.*

6.   *The 1930's. The first match was held in 1932.*

7.   *1986.*

8.   *In case of a tie, the Walker Cup is retained for another two years by the previous winner; the Curtis Cup is held by each country for one year.*

9.   *Charles Seaver. His son Tom won 300 games while pitching for the Mets, Reds, White Sox, and Red Sox.*

U.S. OPEN

1. What golfer has won only three times on the PGA tour and yet has won the U.S. Open twice — once in the 1970's and once in the 1980's?

2. In 1985, when he won, three foreign-born players finished one stroke behind. Give one of them.

3. What amateur finished in second place at an Open during the 1960's?

4. In 1929, Bobby Jones and Al Espinosa tied after 72 holes and played a 36 hole playoff the next day. By how many strokes did Jones win?

5. Probably the most famous U.S. Open of all time took place in 1913 when this American beat two of the best British players in a playoff at Brookline. Who was he?

6. Can you name one of the British players? Hint: Each won a U.S. Open.

7. Who won the first U.S. Open?

8. What 1965 U.S. Open champion donated his entire first place check to charity?

9. Name the only man in the last eighty years to win the U.S. Open twice at the same course. Do you know the course?

> *It matters not the sacrifice*
> *Which makes the duffer's wife so sore.*
> *I am the captive of my slice*
> *I am the servant of my score.*
>
> *—Grantland Rice*

1. *Andy North. He won the Open in 1978 and 1985. His only other win has been the 1977 Westchester Classic.*

2. *Dave Barr, T.C. Chen, and Denis Watson.*

3. *Jack Nicklaus in 1960. Arnold Palmer beat him.*

4. *23. He won 141-164.*

5. *Francis Ouimet. This Open changed the American public's perception of golf. Previously, golf was considered a foreign game and a rich man's sport until the local twenty-year-old who was a former caddy at Brookline won it.*

6. *Edward "Ted" Ray and Harry Vardon.*

7. *Horace Rawlins.*

8. *Gary Player.*

9. *Jack Nicklaus in 1967 and 1980 at Baltusrol.*

CHIP SHOTS

In 1972, Charles W. Conrose, Sr., was awarded patent number 3,436,151 for a pair of golfer's glasses with lines scratched on the lenses in order to line up putts more accurately. So far as we can tell, the glasses were not a blinding success.

BRITISH OPEN

1. In 1923, he failed to qualify for the Open which was being held at Troon. Fifty years later, with the Open again being held at Troon, he got a hole-in-one on the eighth hole. Name this remarkable American.

2. Who won consecutive British Opens in the 1960's?

3. What amateur has won the most British Opens?

4. The first five British Opens played in England were played at two courses. Give one of them.

5. The lowest score ever shot in a round is 63. Name one of the three men to do this.

6. What American has won exactly four British Opens?

7. In the 1980's, two Britishers won their home Open. Give them both.

8. In 1966, for the first time, the British Open was scheduled for four days. Name the American who won.

9. What Australian won three consecutive British Opens during the 1950's?

Through years of experience, I have found that air offers less resistance than dirt. —*Jack Nicklaus, on why he likes to tee the ball high*

1. *Gene Sarazen who was 71 years old when he got that ace.*

2. *Arnold Palmer — in 1961 and 1962.*

3. *Bobby Jones. He won in 1926, 1927, and 1930.*

4. *Royal Liverpool Golf Club in Hoylake and Royal St. George's Golf Club in Sandwich.*

5. *Mark Hayes at Turnberry in 1977; Isao Aoki at Muirfield in 1980; and Greg Norman at Turnberry in 1986.*

6. *Walter Hagen in 1922, 1924, 1928, and 1929.*

7. *Sandy Lyle in 1985 and Nick Faldo in 1987.*

8. *Jack Nicklaus.*

9. *Peter Thomson, 1952 to 1954.*

GEOGRAPHY

1. Which U.S. State has the most golf courses?

2. Which state has the least?

3. Besides Antartica, which continent has the least golfers and the fewest golf courses?

4. The United States has the most golfers in the world. Which country has the second most?

5. Who am I? I hit a golf ball which was out of this world.

6. What South American country has the world's highest course?

7. True or False: The People's Republic of China does not have a single golf course.

8. What member of the PGA Hall of Fame was born in Latrobe, PA?

9. Name the three countries in which the British Open has been held.

It's still embarrassing. I asked my caddie for a sand wedge, and 10 minutes later he came back with a ham on rye. —**Chi Chi Rodriguez,** *talking about his accent*

1. *Florida. California is close behind.*

2. *Alaska.*

3. *South America.*

4. *Japan.*

5. *Astronaut Alan Shepard. He hit a golf ball on the moon in 1971.*

6. *Peru.*

7. *False.*

8. *Arnold Palmer.*

9. *Scotland, England, and Ireland.*

CHIP SHOTS

Tennis star Althea Gibson took up golf in the early 1960's and became the first black member of the LPGA in 1964.

PGA TOUR

1. What is the record for the lowest score in a round in a PGA event?

2. Who shot it?

3. At what tournament was this accomplished?

4. Who was the oldest winner of a PGA event?

5. Greg Norman and Mark O'Meara set an unofficial record for the fastest round in a PGA tournament when they played the 1988 Nabisco Championship at Pebble Beach Golf Links in how many minutes?

6. In 1979, Sam Trahan and, in 1987, Mike McGee set the record for fewest putts in a round. How many?

7. Who holds the PGA record for consecutive wins?

8. How many did he win in a row?

9. Who is the PGA Tour Commissioner?

I never wanted to be a millionaire. I just wanted to live like one.   *—Walter Hagen*

1. *59.*

2. *Al Geiberger. He had six pars, eleven birdies, and one eagle. He shot 29 on the front and 30 on the back nine.*

3. *The 1977 Danny Thomas Memphis Open held at the Colonial Country Club.*

4. *Sam Snead. He was almost 53 when he won the 1965 Greensboro Open.*

5. *84. They ran between shots to set the record. Each shot a 79 that day.*

6. *18.*

7. *Byron Nelson in 1945.*

8. *Eleven.*

9. *Deane Beman.*

RULES

Do you know the rules for each of the following situations? Assume stroke play.

A live bug is crawling on your ball. You mark your ball, pick it up, blow the bug off, and replace your ball. What is the penalty, if any, if your ball was —

1.   on the putting green?

2.   in the fairway?

3.   in a sand trap?

You're on the first tee, ready to make your first shot of the day. What's the call if you —

4.   accidentally knock the ball off the tee as you're addressing it?

5.   address the ball, swing at it, and miss it completely?

6.   address the ball, swing at it, miss it completely, and then inadvertantly knock the ball off the tee as you're addressing it again?

You and I are playing a match. You putt your ball and it hits a caddie. What's the call if the caddie is —

7.   my caddie?

8.   your caddie?

9.   a caddie which we're sharing?

Never have so many spent so much to sit in relative comfort to brag about their failures.
                                        —Keith Jackson

1. *No penalty.*

2. *One stroke penalty.*

3. *Two stroke penalty.*

4. *No stroke — no penalty. You may re-tee the ball.*

5. *The miss counts as a stroke. There is no penalty.*

6. *You get a stroke for the miss and a penalty stroke for moving the ball after it's "in play." You must play the next shot with your ball on the ground and it will be your third stroke.*

7. *No penalty. You may accept the stroke and let the ball lie where it is or cancel the stroke, return the ball to its original position and retake the shot.*

8. *Two stroke penalty and you play the ball where it lies. In a serious situation such as if you have a three stroke lead on the last hole and your caddie stops the ball near the hole when it might have rolled into a lake, disqualification is possible.*

9. *If we are sharing a caddie, he is considered to be your caddie when you are hitting. Consequently, we would follow the rules described in number 8 above.*

Thoughts of the Throne

An exhausted Fuzzy Zoeller, after 36 holes on the final rain-delayed day of the 1981 Colonial National Invitation tournament said, "It was a very long day. I don't know how long we've been out here, but I know it's time to shave again."

LPGA

1. What four events make up the Women's Grand Slam?

2. Who was the first foreigner to win a million dollars on the LPGA Tour?

3. Only one amateur has ever won the U.S. Women's Open. Can you think of her?

4. The LPGA record for most tournaments won in a year is 13. By whom?

5. In 1978, she won two tournaments in a row, did not enter the next tournament, and then won the next three in a row. Who?

6. What is the last name of the golfer known by the first name "Muffin"?

7. This golfer thought she had won the 1957 Women's Open but turned in a signed scorecard with an incorrect score and was disqualified. Who is she?

8. Why was she disqualified?

9. Who has been the leading money winner on the LPGA Tour a record eight times?

Golf is not a game of great shots. It's a game of the most accurate misses. The people who win make the smallest mistakes. —*Gene Littler*

1. *Nabisco Dinah Shore, U.S. Women's Open, duMaurier Classic (in Canada), and LPGA Championship.*

2. *Jan Stephenson.*

3. *Catherine Lacoste in 1967.*

4. *Mickey Wright in 1963.*

5. *Nancy Lopez.*

6. *Spencer-Devlin.*

7. *Jackie Pung.*

8. *The score which she recorded for one hole was lower than what she actually got.*

9. *Kathy Whitworth.*

WHAT'S IN A NAME?

The number 1 wood is still called the driver by most players. Match the club on the left with its modern day counterpart on the right.

1.	Baffy	a.	2 wood
2.	Brassie	b.	3 wood
3.	Cleek	c.	4 wood
4.	Jigger	d.	5 wood
5.	Lofter	e.	3 iron
6.	Mashie	f.	4 iron
7.	Mid Mashie	g.	5 iron
8.	Niblick	h.	8 iron
9.	Spoon	i.	9 iron

Give me a millionaire with a bad backswing and I can have a very pleasant afternoon. **—George Low**

1.   *d.   Baffy = 5 wood.*

2.   *a.   Brassie = 2 wood.*

3.   *c.   Cleek = 4 wood.*

4.   *f.   Jigger = 4 iron.*

5.   *h.   Lofter = 8 iron.*

6.   *g.   Mashie = 5 iron.*

7.   *e.   Mid Mashie = 3 iron.*

8.   *i.   Niblick = 9 iron.*

9.   *b.   Spoon = 3 wood.*

Some other names include: Driving Iron = 1 iron; Midiron = 2 iron; Spade Mashie = 6 iron; and Mashie Niblick = 7 iron.

CHIP SHOTS

According to *Golf Digest*, the odds against an average golfer making an ace are 10,738 to one. On the PGA tour, the odds against a pro making it are 3,708 to one. And on the LPGA circuit the chance is one in 4,648.

U.S. OPEN

1. In 1988, the United States Post Office came out with a stamp honoring a U.S. Open winner. Who?

2. In the same round of the 1989 Open at Oak Hill, four players accomplished something at the sixth hole which had been done only seventeen times previously in the history of the Open. What did they do?

3. Name one of these four players.

4. Who was the first amateur to win the U.S. Open?

5. Within the past sixty years, the biggest margin of victory at the Open in regulation play has been seven strokes. What British golfer did this?

6. What golfer within the last twenty years won the U.S. Open by beating his opponent by eight strokes in a playoff?

7. Who is the only man to win the U.S. Open in three different decades?

8. Besides him, name two of the other three men who have won four U.S. Opens.

9. Give the family name of the three brothers who finished in the top 3 thirteen times and won three U.S. Opens. Hint: Their first names are Willie, Alex, and Macdonald.

Golf is a good walk spoiled. —*Mark Twain*

1.   *Francis Ouimet.*

2.   *Each got a hole-in-one.*

3.   *Jerry Pate, Nick Price, Doug Weaver, and Mark Wiebe. (Each used a seven iron on the 167 yard par 3 hole.)*

4.   *Francis Ouimet in 1913.*

5.   *Tony Jacklin in 1970. He shot a 281 while Dave Hill finished in second place with a 288.*

6.   *Fuzzy Zoeller. He defeated Greg Norman 67-75 for the 1984 Open.*

7.   *Jack Nicklaus.*

8.   *Willie Anderson — 1901, 1903, 1904, 1905; Bobby Jones — 1923, 1926, 1929, 1930; Ben Hogan — 1948, 1950, 1951, 1953.*

9.   *Smith. Willie won in 1899; Alex won in 1906 and 1910; Macdonald tied for the lead in 1910 but lost the playoff.*

THE MASTERS

1. What golfer never won the Masters but finished second four times?

2. The youngest man ever to win the tournament won it four days after his twenty-third birthday. Name him.

3. The oldest person to win was twice as old. Can you think of him?

4. Name one of the three golfers who won the tournament exactly three times.

5. Who has gotten 12 eagles at the Masters?

6. What player lost two Masters playoffs? Hint: He lost to Byron Nelson and Sam Snead.

7. In 1965, this man beat the field by nine strokes. Who is he and can you name one of the two men who finished in second place?

8. Who am I? In 1979, I won the first sudden death playoff in Masters history.

9. Name one of the two men who lost the 1979 sudden death playoff.

We have 51 golf courses in Palm Springs. He never decides which course he will play until after his first tee shot. —*Bob Hope,*
about former President Gerald Ford

1.   *Tom Weiskopf. He finished second in 1969, 1972, 1974, and 1975.*

2.   *Seve Ballesteros in 1980.*

3.   *46-year-old Jack Nicklaus (in 1986).*

4.   *Jimmy Demaret in 1940, '47, and '50; Sam Snead in 1949, '52, and '54; Gary Player in 1961, '74, and '78.*

5.   *Jack Nicklaus.*

6.   *Ben Hogan. He lost to Nelson in 1942 and to Snead in 1954.*

7.   *Jack Nicklaus. He shot a 271 while Arnold Palmer and Gary Player each shot 280 to finish in second place.*

8.   *Fuzzy Zoeller.*

9.   *Ed Sneed and Tom Watson.*

Thoughts of the Throne

Lee Trevino, talking of the similar roots he and Seve Ballesteros share, once said, "We come from the same backgrounds, more or less, where growing up next to a golf course didn't mean a 10,000-square foot house and gold faucets in the bathrooms."

FOREIGN-BORN

Identify the native countries of these players.

1. Ian Baker-Finch

2. Bob Charles

3. Bruce Crampton

4. Roberto DeVicenzo

5. Bruce Devlin

6. George Knudson

7. Gary Player

8. Peter Thomson

9. Ian Woosman

I shot a wild elephant in Africa 30 yards from me, and it didn't hit the ground until it was right at my feet. I wasn't a bit scared. But a 4-foot putt scares me to death.   **—Sam Snead**

1. *Australia.*

2. *New Zealand.*

3. *Australia.*

4. *Argentina.*

5. *Australia.*

6. *Canada.*

7. *South Africa.*

8. *Australia.*

9. *Wales.*

MAJORS

1. There have been four players with ten or more letters in their last names who have won professional Majors within the past sixty years. Name two of them.

2. Which of the four modern Grand Slam events has the smallest field of players?

3. How many professional Majors has Jack Nicklaus won?

4. Can you name them?

5. What other Major has he won twice?

6. Numerous players have won two professional Majors in the same year. Name the two players who accomplished this in the 1980's.

7. Who was the last man to win three of the professional Majors in the same year?

8. A tie after regulation is broken by an immediate sudden-death playoff in which two Grand Slam events?

9. Of all the players to ever win a Major, alphabetically who comes first?

The only problem with the Senior Tour is that when you're through there, they put you in a box.
—J.C. Snead

1.   *Seve Ballesteros, Mark Calcavecchia, Dow Finster-*
     wald, and Cary Middlecoff.

2.   *The Masters.*

3.   *Eighteen.*

4.   *Three British Opens, four U.S. Opens, five PGA*
     Championships, and six Masters.

5.   *The U.S. Amateur.*

6.   *Jack Nicklaus in 1980 and Tom Watson in 1982.*

7.   *Ben Hogan in 1953.*

8.   *The Masters and the PGA Championship.*

9.   *Tommy Aaron.*

CHIP SHOTS

At the Port Royal Golf Course in Bermuda on March 27, 1975, twenty-one-year-old Joe Flynn recorded the lowest 18 hole score ever, an 82. Not up to par, you say? Doubting duffers should know that Flynn's course record was for *throwing* the ball.

COURSES

The following courses hosted at least two U.S. Opens since 1950. Name the state in which each is located. For extra credit, give each locality as well.

1. Cherry Hills Country Club

2. Inverness Club

3. Merion Golf Club

4. Oak Hill Country Club

5. Oakland Hills Country Club

6. Oakmont Country Club

7. Olympic Club

8. Southern Hills Country Club

9. Winged Foot Golf Club

I don't trust doctors. They are like golfers. Every one has a different answer to your problem.
—Seve Ballesteros

1. *Englewood, Colorado.*

2. *Toledo, Ohio.*

3. *Ardmore, Pennsylvania.*

4. *Rochester, New York.*

5. *Birmingham, Michigan.*

6. *Oakmont, Pennsylvania.*

7. *San Francisco, California.*

8. *Tulsa, Oklahoma.*

9. *Mamaroneck, New York.*

POTPOURRI

1. In 1981, the United States Post Office came out with a stamp honoring this male Hall of Fame golfer. Can you name him?

2. At the same time, they came out with a stamp honoring a female Hall of Fame golfer. Do you know her?

3. The king of what country banned golf in 1457?

4. The son of what Cy Young Award winner for baseball has won more than a half million dollars on the PGA Tour?

5. Talking about baseball, what American League RBI leader retired from baseball and tried to make it on the PGA Tour but was unsuccessful?

6. Who is the only man to shoot 15 under par in a 72 hole PGA event without shooting a round in the 60's?

7. What is a stymie?

8. Is a stymie legal?

9. Who is the only man to get a double eagle in the last fifty years at the Masters?

I find it to be the hole in one.

—Groucho Marx,
when asked about
golf's most difficult shot

1. *Bobby Jones.*

2. *Babe Zaharias.*

3. *King James II of Scotland. The ban lasted until 1502.*

4. *Jim Perry. His son is Chris Perry.*

5. *Ken Harrelson in 1972.*

6. *Al Geiberger.*

7. *An intentional putt between an opponent's ball and the hole without marking the ball. Thus, the opponent is forced to putt around the ball.*

8. *Not any longer; it was outlawed in 1951.*

9. *Bruce Devlin in 1967.*

Thoughts of the Throne

Real golfers don't go in the bushes.   *—Bob Kunstel*

ALL BUT ONE

Each of the following players has won three of the four professional Majors. Name the one that he did not win.

1. Tommy Armour

2. Jim Barnes

3. Raymond Floyd

4. Walter Hagen

5. Byron Nelson

6. Arnold Palmer

7. Sam Snead

8. Lee Trevino

9. Tom Watson

When your name is Zoeller, and so many things are done in alphabetical order, you expect to be last.
—Fuzzy Zoeller

1. *The Masters.*

2. *The Masters.*

3. *The British Open.*

4. *The Masters.*

5. *The British Open.*

6. *The PGA Championship.*

7. *The U.S. Open.*

8. *The Masters.*

9. *The PGA Championship.*

It should be noted that Tommy Armour, Jim Barnes, and Walter Hagen were past their primes when the Masters was originated.

The Bathroom Library

For further information, write to:
Red-Letter Press, Inc.
P.O. Box 393,
Saddle River, N.J. 07458